At Sylvan, we believe reading is one of life's most important and enriching abilities, and we're glad you've chosen our resources to help your child build this critically important skill. We know that the time you spend with your child reinforcing the lessons learned in school will contribute to his or her love of reading. This love of reading will translate into academic achievement. Successful readers are ready for the world around them; they are prepared to do research, to experience literature, and to make the connections necessary to achieve in school and life.

In teaching reading at Sylvan, we use a research-based, step-by-step process, which includes thought-provoking reading selections and activities. Our Sylvan workbooks are designed to help you to help your child build the skills and confidence that will contribute to his or her success in school. Let us partner with you to support the development of a confident, well-prepared, independent learner.

The Sylvan Team

Kindergarten
Success with Sight Words
Workbook

Published in the United States by Random House, Inc., New York, and in Canada by Random House of Canada Limited, Toronto.

www.tutoring.sylvanlearning.com

Created by Smarterville Productions LLC
Producer & Editorial Direction: The Linguistic Edge
Producer: TJ Trochlil McGreevy
Writer: Christina Wilsdon
Cover and Interior Illustrations: Shawn Finley, Tim Goldman, and Duendes del Sur
Layout and Art Direction: SunDried Penguin

First Edition

ISBN: 978-0-307-47931-0
ISSN: 2156-6275

This book is available at special discounts for bulk purchases for sales promotions or premiums. For more information, write to Special Markets/Premium Sales, 1745 Broadway, MD 6-2, New York, New York 10019 or e-mail specialmarkets@randomhouse.com.

PRINTED IN THE UNITED STATES

20 19 18 17 16 15 14 13

Contents

Space Trace

Space Ace found words in the stars! TRACE the words so he can read them.

  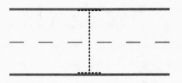

 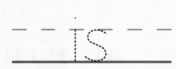 

Say It

LOOK at the words. READ each word out loud. Then READ each word out loud again in a super-quiet voice.

Spot the Dots

READ each word in the box. LOOK for only those words in the picture. DRAW a line to connect the words in ABC order, as they appear in the box. FIND the mystery picture!

HINT: It is crunchy and sweet and good to eat.

a	am	are	I	is	the

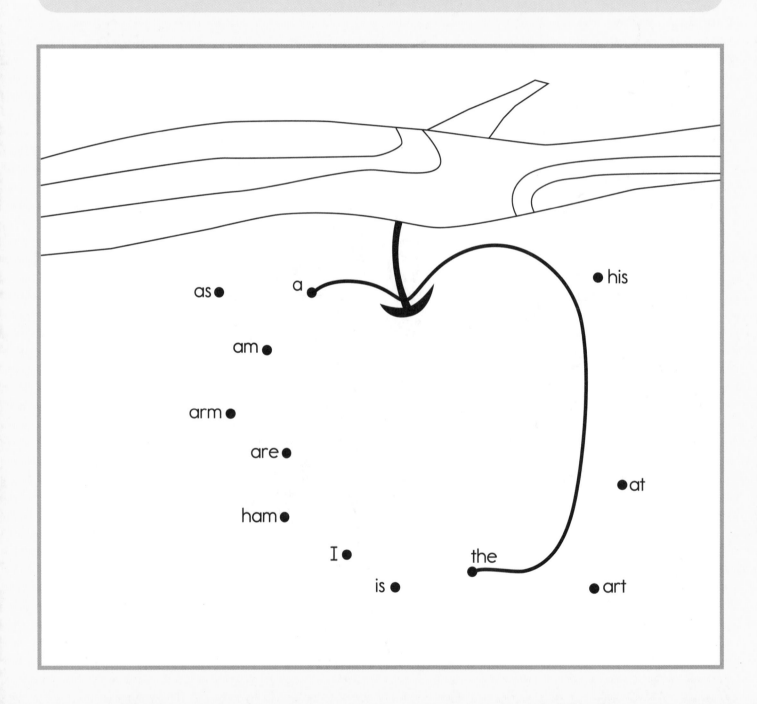

Word Blocks

SAY the words. FILL IN each word block with a word of the same shape.

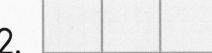

1.

2.

3.

4.

5.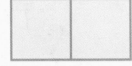

6.

Jiffy Words

Blank Out

READ each word. LOOK at each picture. WRITE the word to complete each sentence.

HINT: Each word is used only once.

am	are	a	is

I see _____ blue bird.
1

The flower _____ red.
2

The balloons _____ green.
3

I _____ in the bed.
4

Start Your Crayons!

READ the words. COLOR only the dinosaurs that are wearing the words from the box.

a	the	I	am	is	are

Blank Out

READ each word. LOOK at each picture. WRITE the word to complete each sentence.

HINT: Each word is used only once.

see	find	run	come	can

I _____ fast.
1

The pig _____ fly!
2

Do not let the dog _____ in.
3

Help me _____ my shoe.
4

I _____ a bear.
5

Poetry Guy

Help Poetry Guy write his poems. READ the words. FILL IN words that rhyme.

come	see	run	can

It is lots of fun

to _____.
₁

I can _____
₂

a busy bee.

Will you _____?
₃

I have some gum!

My hat _____
₄

fit in a pan.

Match It

READ each word. DRAW a line from each word to the correct picture.

find

see

run

come

Story Time

READ the words. Then READ the story. CIRCLE the words as you find them.

| can | see | run | come | find |

I come home from school.

I run into the house.

I see a box!

I find my name on it.

Yay!

I can open the box!

Word Hunt

READ the words. CIRCLE the words in the grid. WRITE each word after you circle it. Words go across and down.

| run | see | can | find | come |

```
i  q  r  c  f
s  s  u  o  i
c  a  n  m  n
s  e  e  e  d
```

_____   _____   _____
- - - - - - - -   - - - - - - - -   - - - - - - - -
_____   _____   _____

              _____   _____
              - - - - - - - -   - - - - - - - -
              _____   _____

Meet in the Middle

Can you help these kids get to the middle of the maze? READ the word each kid is wearing. FIND the words in the maze. DRAW a line through the words to get to the middle.

What's It Like?

Space Trace

Space Ace found words in the stars! TRACE the words so he can read them.

big   little   long

old   pretty

Start Your Crayons!

READ the words. COLOR only the dinosaurs that are wearing the words from the box.

| big | little | long | old | pretty |

Blank Out

READ each word. LOOK at each picture. WRITE the word to complete each sentence.

HINT: Each word is used only once.

| big | little | long | pretty |

The elephant is _____.
1

The mouse is very _____.
2

The flower is _____.
3

The line is very _____.
4

Stop, Drop, and Draw

READ each sentence. DRAW a picture to match each sentence.

Here is a pretty bird.

That is a big shoe!

Look at the long snake.

See the old house.

Word Hunt

READ the words. CIRCLE the words in the grid. WRITE each word after you circle it.
Words go across and down.

is   old   see   come   run   big   am   long

i	o	l	d	s
s	c	o	m	e
r	u	n	a	e
b	i	g	m	f

Word Blocks

SAY the words. FILL IN each word block with a word of the same shape.

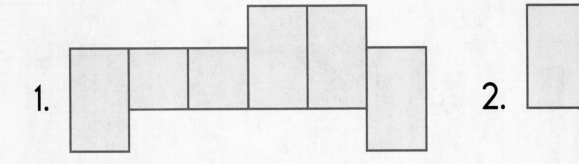

the   find   can   little   pretty   I

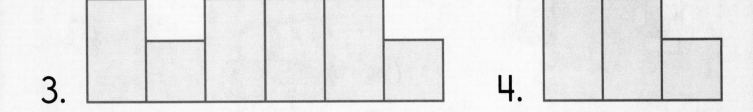

1.

2.

3.

4.

5.

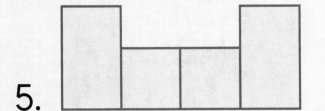

6.

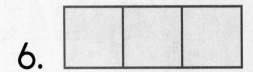

Hide and Speak

READ each color word out loud. DRAW a line from each color word to a car in the picture that matches it.

red   blue   yellow   green   brown   black

Name It

LOOK at each picture. READ the words next to the picture. CIRCLE the word that matches the picture.

   bed   red   rod

   blue   boo   bird

   pink   red   yellow

   gray   green   grow

   brown   bow   town

   back   block   black

Colorful Words

Match It

READ each word. DRAW a line from each word to the correct picture.

red

blue

yellow

green

brown

black

Blank Out

READ each word. LOOK at each picture. WRITE the word to complete each sentence.

| red | blue | yellow | green | brown | black |

I see a _____ bird.
1

My dress is _____.
2

Here is a _____ horse.
3

I love the _____ sun.
4

The leaf is _____.
5

The bug is _____.
6

Colorful Words

Start Your Crayons!

READ the words. COLOR only the dinosaurs that are wearing the words from the box—and make the colors match the words too!

red   blue   yellow   green   brown   black

Stop, Drop, and Draw

READ each sentence. DRAW a picture to match each sentence.

I have a green hat.

She has blue shoes.

The fish is red.

I see a brown bear.

Tag It

TRACE the words. DRAW a line from each word to the animal it matches in the picture.

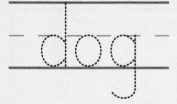

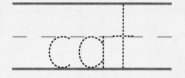

rabbit

fish

Name It

LOOK at each picture. READ the words next to the picture. CIRCLE the word that matches the picture.

dig   dog   hog

cat   cut   rat

robot   rabbit   rub

bad   bat   bird

fish   dish   fun

Story Time

READ the words. Then READ the story. CIRCLE the words as you find them.

| cat | dog | fish | bird | rabbit |

The dog took a bath.

The cat took a bath.

So did the rabbit.

The bird did too.

"Please get out of my bowl," said the fish.

Match It

READ each word. DRAW a line from each word to the correct picture.

dog

cat

rabbit

bird

fish

Stop, Drop, and Draw

READ each sentence. DRAW a picture to match each sentence.

My dog has long ears.

That cat can fly.

I see a green rabbit.

A fish is in my bed!

Spot the Dots

READ each word in the box. LOOK for only those words in the picture. DRAW a line to connect the words in ABC order, as they appear in the box. FIND the mystery picture!

HINT: This little pet likes to get wet.

bird	cat	dog	fish	rabbit

dish

dig

rat

dog

mat

dug

fish

cat

rabbit

bud

bird

wish

Space Trace

Space Ace found words in the stars! TRACE the words so he can read them.

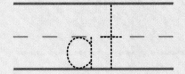

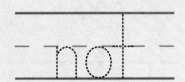

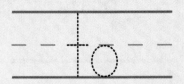

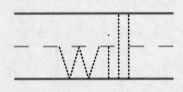

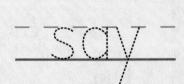

Say It

LOOK at the words. READ each word out loud. Then READ each word out loud again, but this time clap after each word.

at

not

to

an

will

say

Word Blocks

SAY the words. FILL IN each word block with a word of the same shape.

| at | not | to | an | will | say |

1.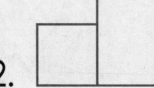

2.

3.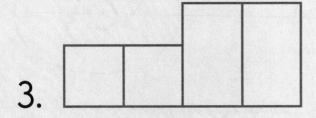

4.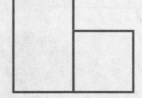

5.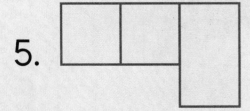

6.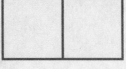

Blank Out

READ each word. LOOK at each picture. WRITE the word to complete each sentence.

HINT: Each word is used only once.

will	to	not	an

I do _____ like rain.
₁

He gave the box _____ the girl.
₂

The baby _____ cry if you go.
₃

The boy ate _____ apple.
₄

Start Your Crayons!

READ the words. COLOR only the dinosaurs that are wearing the words from the box.

at	not	to	an	will	say

Meet in the Middle

Can you help these kids get to the middle of the maze? READ the word each kid is wearing. FIND the words in the maze. DRAW a line through the words to get to the middle.

Space Trace

Space Ace found words in the stars! TRACE the words so he can read them.

he   she   it

you   me   we

Word Blocks

SAY the words. FILL IN each word block with a word of the same shape.

he	she	it	you	me

1.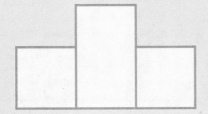

2.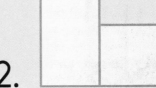

3.

4.

5.

39

Word Hunt

READ the words. CIRCLE the words in the grid. WRITE each word after you circle it. Words go across and down.

he   she   it   you   me   we

```
i   t   m
s   h   e
w   e   r
y   o   u
```

_____   _____   _____

- - - - - - - -   - - - - - - - -   - - - - - - - -

_____   _____   _____

- - - - - - - -   - - - - - - - -   - - - - - - - -

_____   _____   _____

Spot the Dots

READ each word in the box. LOOK for only those words in the picture. DRAW a line to connect the words in ABC order, as they appear in the box. FIND the mystery picture!

HINT: You and me—we need this for tea!

he	it	me	she	we	you

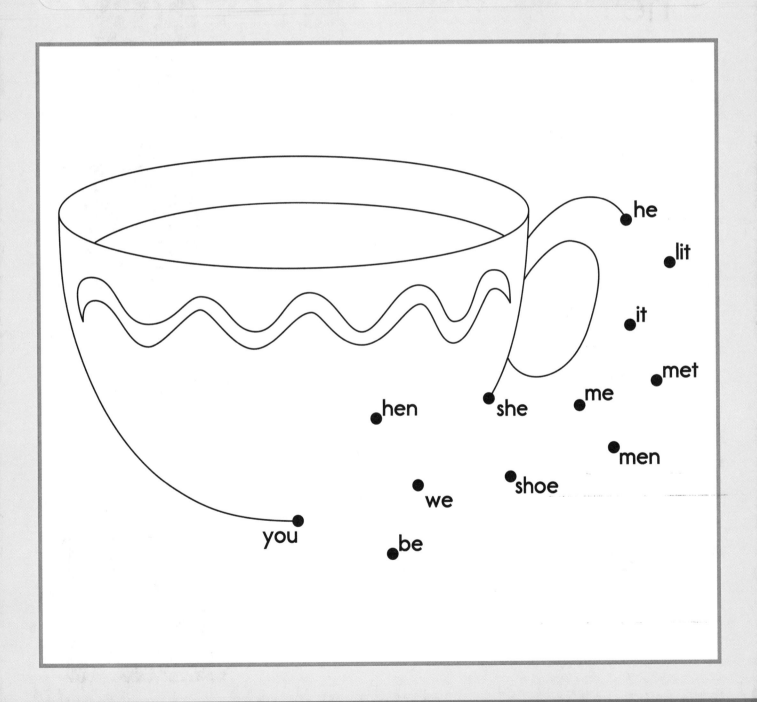

Match It

READ each word. DRAW a line from each word to the correct picture.

he

it

she

we

Meet in the Middle

Can you help these kids get to the middle of the maze? READ the word each kid is wearing. FIND the words in the maze. DRAW a line through the words to get to the middle.

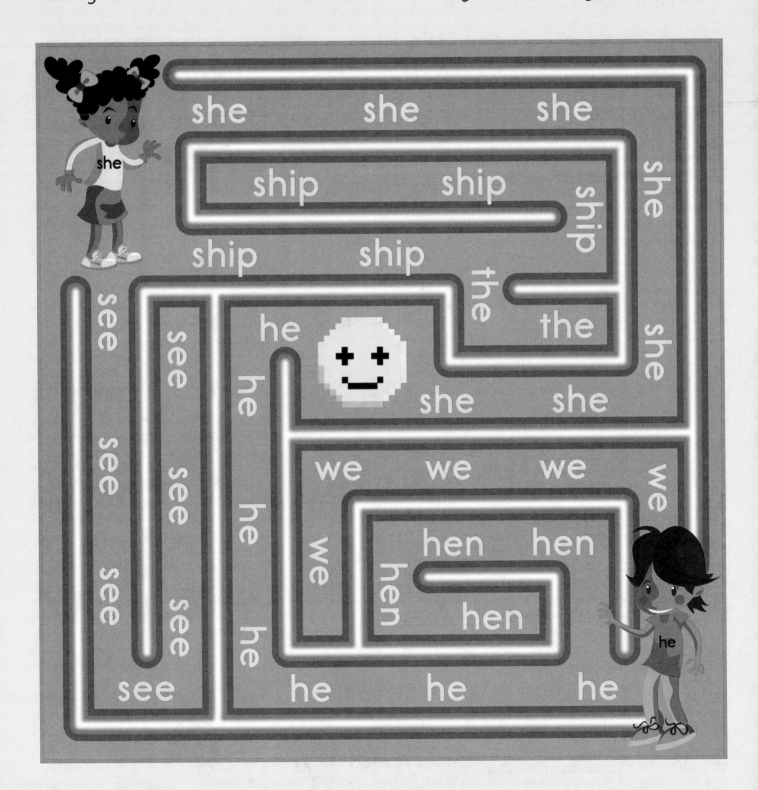

Blank Out

READ each word. LOOK at each picture. WRITE the word to complete each sentence.

HINT: Each word is used only once.

a	you	are	green	fish

The alligator is _____.
1

Sue, _____ you OK?
2

This bike is for _____.
3

That is a big _____.
4

I see _____ butterfly.
5

Try to Remember

CUT OUT the cards. READ the rules. PLAY the game!

Rules: Two players
1. MIX UP the cards.
2. PLACE the cards face down on a table.
3. TAKE TURNS turning over two cards at a time.
4. KEEP the cards when you match two words.

How many matches can you collect?

me	me	he	he
are	are	an	an
you	you	will	will
to	to	the	the

Word Hunt

READ the words. CIRCLE the words in the grid. WRITE each word after you circle it.
Words go across and down.

| rabbit | not | say | you | green | are | big | she |

x	g	r	e	e	n
a	s	h	e	b	o
r	a	b	b	i	t
e	y	o	u	g	m

47

Match It

READ each word. DRAW a line from each word to the correct number.

five

six

two

four

one

three

1

2

3

4

5

6

Name It

LOOK at each number. READ the words next to the number. CIRCLE the word that matches the number.

1   won   one   on

2   to   top   two

3   three   tree   two

4   for   fur   four

5   hive   five   fit

6   six   sick   sacks

Count on It!

Blank Out

READ each word. LOOK at each picture. WRITE the word to complete each sentence.

HINT: Each word is used only once.

one	two	three	four	five	six

The doll has _____ shoes.
1

An ant has _____ legs.
2

I blew _____ bubble.
3

The giraffe has _____ legs.
4

A hand has _____ fingers.
5

Here are _____ paintbrushes.
6

Spot the Dots

READ each word in the box. LOOK for only those words in the picture. DRAW a line to connect the words in 1-2-3 order to find the mystery picture.

HINT: This thing can ring—and even sing!

| one | two | three | four | five | six |

two

tow

tree

one

for

fur

three

too

six

four

sits

hive

five

Tag It

TRACE the words. DRAW a line from each word to something it matches in the picture.

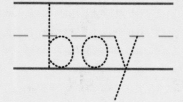

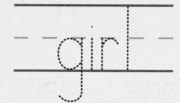

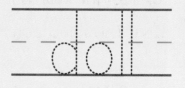

Start Your Crayons!

READ the words. COLOR only the dinosaurs that are wearing the words from the box.

| boy | girl | toy | doll | ball |

Blank Out

READ each word. LOOK at each picture. WRITE the word to complete each sentence.

HINT: Each word is used only once.

| boy | girl | toy | doll | ball |

The _____ has green hair.
1

A _____ is round.
2

See the _____ jump.
3

The _____ yells.
4

A top is a kind of _____.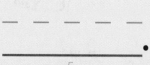
5

Spot the Dots

READ each word in the box. LOOK for only those words in the picture. DRAW a line to connect the words in ABC order, as they appear in the box. FIND the mystery picture!

HINT: This one likes to play all day!

ball	boy	doll	girl	toy

bay•

buy•

ball•

fall•

gill•

boy•

doll•

wall•

girl•

toy•

roll•

Say It

LOOK at the words. READ each word out loud. Then READ each word out loud again in a funny voice.

Word Blocks

SAY the words. FILL IN each word block with a word of the same shape.

go	get	play	ride	work

1.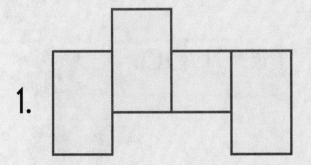

2.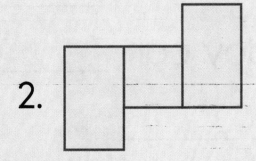

3.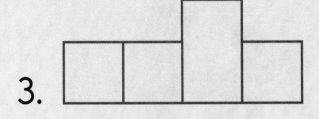

4.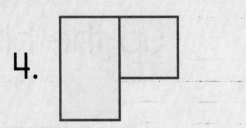

5.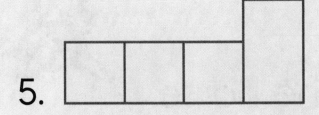

Blank Out

READ each word. LOOK at each picture. WRITE the word to complete each sentence.

HINT: Each word is used only once.

go	get	play	ride	work

The boy can _____ the tuba.
1

I will _____ the red hat.
2

I _____ up the hill.
3

This is hard _____!
4

See the girl _____ the horse.
5

Poetry Guy

Help Poetry Guy write his poems. READ the words. FILL IN words that rhyme.

get	ride	go	play

Will you _____ to see the show?
1

I like to _____ every day.
2

You will _____ very wet!
3

I do not _____ a horse inside.
4

Match It

READ each word. DRAW a line from each word to the correct picture.

go

ride

play

work

Meet in the Middle

Can you help these kids get to the middle of the maze? READ the word each kid is wearing. FIND the words in the maze. DRAW a line through the words to get to the middle.

Order Up!

MATCH each picture with a sentence. WRITE the number of the picture next to the sentence it matches. Now READ the story in the correct order.

1.

2.

3.

4.

Now we can play!

Get the brown rabbit.

Get the red toy.

Get the big ball.

Story Time

READ the words. Then READ the story. CIRCLE the words as you find them.

| ball | boy | will | say | cat | toy | dog |
| rabbit | fish | girl | big | play | little | |

The little girl has a rabbit.

The boy has a toy.

The big dog has a ball.

The cat has a fish.

"Will you play?" they say.

Yes!

Tag It

TRACE the words. DRAW a line from each word to the part of the picture it matches.

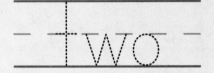

two

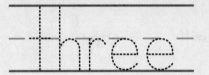

three

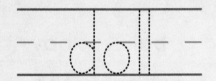

doll

ball

girl

five

Word Hunt

READ the words. CIRCLE the words in the grid. WRITE each word after you circle it. Words go across and down.

| boy | two | toy | doll | play | get | go | red | six | she |

s	i	x	r	e	d
h	g	e	t	w	o
e	o	b	o	y	l
p	l	a	y	l	l

- - - - - -

- - - - - -

- - - - - -

- - - - - -

Even More Busy Words

Say It

LOOK at the words. READ each word out loud. Then READ each word out loud again in a "parrot" voice. Squawk!

11

Blank Out

READ each word. LOOK at each picture. WRITE the word to complete each sentence.

HINT: Each word is used only once.

give	want	like	look	make

See Dad _____ a cake.
1

I will _____ you some pizza.
2

I _____ in the mirror!
3

I _____ my cat.
4

Do you _____ some mud?
5

Even More Busy Words

Start Your Crayons!

READ the words. COLOR only the dinosaurs that are wearing the words from the box.

give   want   like   look   make

Word Blocks

SAY the words. FILL IN each word block with a word of the same shape.

| give | want | look | like | make |

1.

2.

3.

4.

5.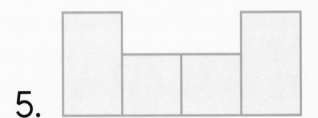

Match It

READ each word. DRAW a line from each word to the correct picture.

egg

cake

milk

soup

banana

apple

Hide and Speak

READ each word out loud. DRAW a line from each word to a food in the kitchen that matches it.

egg   cake   milk   soup   banana   apple

What's for Lunch?

Order Up!

MATCH each picture with a sentence. WRITE the number of the picture next to the sentence it matches. Now READ the story in the correct order.

He put in milk.

Look! A cake!

I put in an egg.

She put in a banana.

Stop, Drop, and Draw

READ each sentence. DRAW a picture to match each sentence.

The cake is pretty.

Look what was in the egg.

A worm is in the apple.

This is birthday soup.

What's for Lunch?

Tag It

TRACE the words. DRAW a line from each word to something it matches in the picture.

egg   cake   milk

soup   banana   apple

Name It

LOOK at each picture. READ the words next to the picture. CIRCLE the word that matches the picture.

 soap   soup   soak

 apple   ape   happy

 mint   melt   milk

 cook   make   cake

 egg   leg   edge

 band   banana   bandage

Say It

LOOK at the words. READ each word out loud. Then READ each word out loud again, stopping each time to act it out before reading the next word.

Word Blocks

SAY the words. FILL IN each word block with a word of the same shape.

up   down   on   under   out

1.

2.

3.

4.

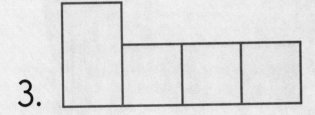

5.

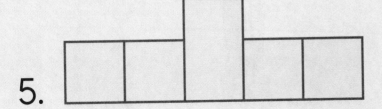

Match It

READ each word. DRAW a line from each word to the correct picture.

HINT: To find the answer, look for the mouse in each picture.

up

down

in

under

Blank Out

READ each word. LOOK at each picture. WRITE the word to complete each sentence.

HINT: Each word is used only once.

| up | down | in | on | under |

The boy went _____ the hill.
1

The ball is _____ the dog.
2

The bug is _____ the net.
3

The cat is _____ the mitten.
4

The van went _____ the hill.
5

Meet in the Middle

Can you help these kids get to the middle of the maze? READ the word each kid is wearing. FIND the words in the maze. DRAW a line through the words to get to the middle.

Order Up!

MATCH each picture with a sentence. WRITE the number of the picture next to the sentence it matches. Now READ the story in the correct order.

The turtle went in the water.

The turtle stuck out his head to say "Good-bye!"

The turtle went under the water.

The bird sat on the turtle.

Name It

LOOK at each picture. READ the words next to the picture. CIRCLE the word that matches the picture.

live   give   go

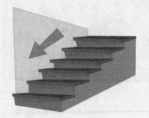

town   dawn   down

look   lock   book

up   pup   under

make   cake   cook

Try to Remember

CUT OUT the cards. READ the rules. PLAY the game!

Rules: Two players
1. MIX UP the cards.
2. PLACE the cards face down on a table.
3. TAKE TURNS turning over two cards at a time.
4. KEEP the cards when you match two words.

How many matches can you collect?

under	under	soup	soup
want	want	like	like
in	in	on	on
give	give	out	out

Poetry Guy

Help Poetry Guy write his poems. READ the words. FILL IN words that rhyme.

like	make	look	under

Can you _____
1

an apple cake?

Please take a _____
2

at my poetry book!

What is _____
3

this rock, I wonder!

I really _____
4

to ride my bike.

85

Say It

LOOK at the words. READ each word out loud. Then READ each word out loud again in a squeaky mouse voice.

Space Trace

Space Ace found words in the stars! TRACE the words so he can read them.

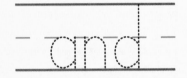

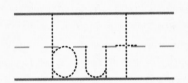

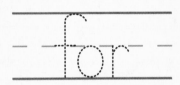

This & That

Word Blocks

SAY the words. FILL IN each word block with a word of the same shape.

| and | but | for | no | yes |

1.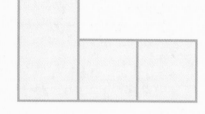

2.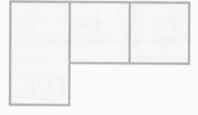

3.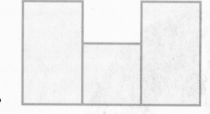

4.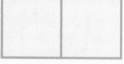

5.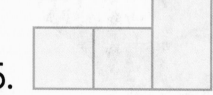

Start Your Crayons!

READ the words. COLOR only the dinosaurs that are wearing the words from the box.

| and | but | for | so | yes | no |

Space Trace

Space Ace found words in the stars! TRACE the words so he can read them.

do   has   have

was   my   be

Blank Out

READ each word. LOOK at each picture. WRITE the word to complete each sentence.

HINT: Each word is used only once.

have	be	has	my	do

I _____ not like big bugs.

I _____ three snakes.

She _____ a hot dog.

This is _____ dog.

Will you _____ my friend?

Match It

READ each sentence. DRAW a line from each sentence to the correct picture.

I have four legs.

She has a doll.

I do not have fur.

Yes, my bird is green.

Poetry Guy

Help Poetry Guy write his poems. READ the words. FILL IN words that rhyme.

do	was	my	be

What can you _____
1

with a kangaroo?

You can have _____
2

apple pie.

My dog likes to _____
3

with me.

What bug _____
4

going "buzz, buzz, buzz"?

Spot the Dots

READ each word in the box. LOOK for only those words in the picture. DRAW a line to connect the words in ABC order, as they appear in the box. FIND the mystery picture!

HINT: I have wings but do not fly. My tummy is white. What am I?

be	do	has	have	my	was

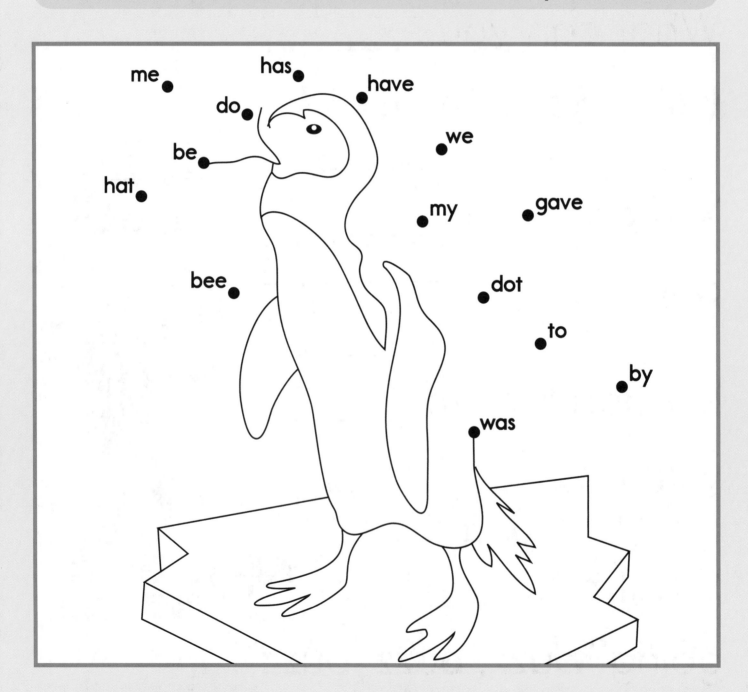

Meet in the Middle

Can you help these kids get to the middle of the maze? READ the word each kid is wearing. FIND the words in the maze. DRAW a line through the words to get to the middle.

Tag It

TRACE the words. DRAW a line from each word to something it matches in the picture.

feet   leg   eyes

hand   head

Name It

LOOK at each picture. READ the words next to the picture. CIRCLE the word that matches the picture.

 foot   feet   fee

 leg   log   beg

 I   eyes   yes

 band   had   hand

head   had   hid

Order Up!

MATCH each picture with a sentence. WRITE the number of the picture next to the sentence it matches. Now READ the story in the correct order.

But only one hand!

I see a head.

I see lots of feet.

I see eyes.

Blank Out

READ each word. LOOK at each picture. WRITE the word to complete each sentence.

HINT: Each word is used only once.

feet	leg	eyes	hand	head

I have two _____.
1

My _____ is wet.
2

I hurt my _____.
3

The cat has four _____.
4

The boy waves his _____.
5

Story Time

READ the words. Then READ the story. CIRCLE the words as you find them.

| feet | leg | eyes | hand | head |

The dog licked my hand.

He sat by my feet.

Then he put his head on my leg.

I looked at his big brown eyes.

I will ask Dad if we can keep him!

Word Hunt

READ the words. CIRCLE the words in the grid. WRITE each word after you circle it. Words go across and down.

| feet | head | leg | eyes | hand |

f	m	l	e	h
e	y	e	s	e
e	h	g	a	a
t	h	a	n	d

_____ _____ _____

_____ _____

Match It

READ each word. DRAW a line from each word to the correct picture.

car

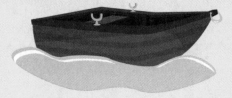

bus

boat

truck

train

plane

Stop, Drop, and Draw

READ each sentence. DRAW a picture to match each sentence.

This car can fly!

I sail my boat.

It's the ice cream truck!

Here is a school bus for fish.

On the Go

Name It

LOOK at each picture. READ the words next to the picture. CIRCLE the word that matches the picture.

   cat   car   can

   bus   but   was

   coat   bit   boat

   trick   tuck   truck

   rain   train   tan

   plane   plan   plate

Order Up!

MATCH each picture with a sentence. WRITE the number of the picture next to the sentence it matches. Now READ the story in the correct order.

The truck went on the train.

But I went on the plane!

The car went on the truck.

The train went on the boat.

On the Go

Hide and Speak

READ each word out loud. DRAW a line from each word to something in the picture that matches it.

car

bus

boat

truck

train

plane

Story Time

READ the words. Then READ the story. CIRCLE the words as you find them.

| car | bus | boat | truck | train | plane |

I put my train in a box.

I put in my plane too.

Then I put in a car and a bus.

Mom put the box on the truck.

"Wait!" I said.

I ran back into the house.

I almost forgot my boat!

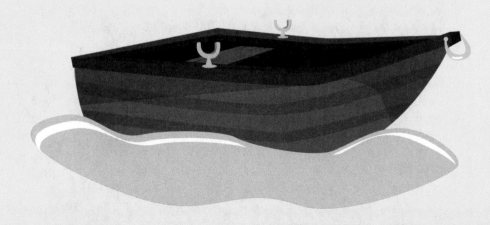

Say It

LOOK at the words. READ each word out loud. Then READ each word out loud again in a spooky voice.

Space Trace

Space Ace found words in the stars! TRACE the words so he can read them.

saw

that

this

said

who

what

Word Blocks

SAY the words. FILL IN each word block with a word of the same shape.

saw   that   said   who   what

1.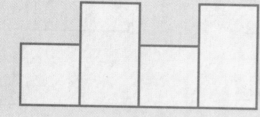

2.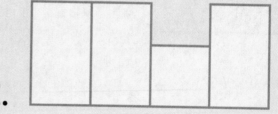

3.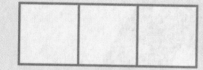

4.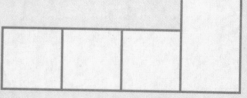

5.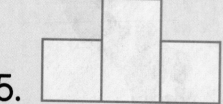

Word Hunt

READ the words. CIRCLE the words in the grid. WRITE each word after you circle it. Words go across and down.

| this | that | said | who | what |

w	w	h	o	t
t	h	i	s	h
s	a	i	d	m
a	t	h	a	t

Blank Out

READ each word. LOOK at each picture. WRITE the word to complete each sentence.

HINT: Each word is used only once.

| saw | what | this | said | who |

I know _____ is at the door!
1

I like _____ ball.
2

She _____ a big bug.
3

"Mine!" _____ the baby.
4

Do you know _____ time it is?
5

Spot the Dots

READ each word in the box. LOOK for only those words in the picture. DRAW a line to connect the words in ABC order, as they appear in the box. FIND the mystery picture!

HINT: "Who" is a word said by this bird.

| said | saw | that | this | what | who |

thin

sad

saw

that

hat

watt

this

was

said

what

wet

how

who

Review

Match It

READ each word. DRAW a line from each word to the correct picture.

egg

leg

train

head

car

Poetry Guy

Help Poetry Guy write his poems. READ the words. FILL IN words that rhyme.

who	that	boat	head

My friend Ned

has five hats on his _____.
1

I wonder _____
2

put an egg in my shoe.

What is _____?
3

Oh! Just a cat!

I have a _____,
4

but it does not float.

Start Your Crayons!

READ the words. COLOR only the dinosaurs that are wearing the words from the box.

what	hand	was	has	bus	head	saw

Try to Remember

CUT OUT the cards. READ the rules. PLAY the game!

Rules: Two players

1. MIX UP the cards.
2. PLACE the cards face down on a table.
3. TAKE TURNS turning over two cards at a time.
4. KEEP the cards when you match two words.

How many matches can you collect?

and	and	has	has
was	was	hand	hand
said	said	saw	saw
this	this	that	that

Answers

Page 4

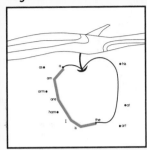

Page 5
1. is 2. are
3. I 4. a
5. am 6. the

Page 6
1. a 2. is
3. are 4. am

Page 7

Page 8
1. run 2. can
3. come 4. find
5. see

Page 9
1. run 2. see
3. come 4. can

Page 10

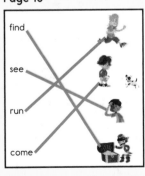

Page 11

I come home from school.
I run into the house.
I see a box!
I find my name on it.
Yay!
I can open the box!

Page 12

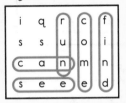

i	q	r	c		f
s	s	u	o		i
c	a	n	m		n
s	e	e			d

Page 13

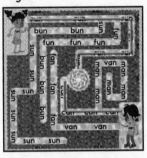

Page 15

Page 16
1. pretty 2. little
3. big 4. long

Page 17
Have someone check
your answers.

Page 18

l	o	l	d	s
s	c	o	m	e
r	u	n	a	e
b	i	g	m	f

Page 19
1. pretty 2. I
3. little 4. the
5. find 6. can

Page 20

red blue yellow green brown black

Page 21

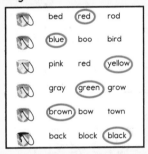

	bed	red	rod
	blue	boo	bird
	pink	red	yellow
	gray	green	grow
	brown	bow	town
	back	block	black

Page 22

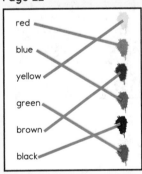

red
blue
yellow
green
brown
black

Page 23
1. blue 2. red
3. black 4. yellow
5. green 6. brown

Page 24

yellow green
true black
red brown
grown blue

Page 25
Have someone check
your answers.

Page 26

dog cat bird
rabbit fish

Page 27

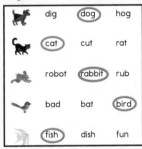

	dig	dog	hog
	cat	cut	rat
	robot	rabbit	rub
	bad	bat	bird
	fish	dish	fun

Page 28

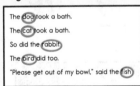

The dog took a bath.
The cat took a bath.
So did the rabbit.
The bird did too.
"Please get out of my bowl," said the fish.

Page 29

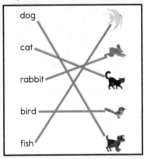

dog
cat
rabbit
bird
fish

Page 30
Have someone check
your answers.

Answers

Page 31
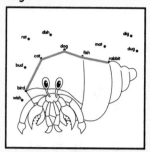

Page 34
1. not   2. at
3. will   4. to
5. say   6. an

Page 35
1. not   2. to
3. will   4. an

Page 36

Page 37
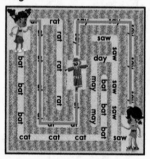

Page 39
1. she   2. he
3. me   4. you
5. it

Page 40

Page 41

Page 42
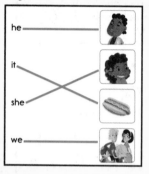

Page 43

Page 44
1. green   2. are
3. you   4. fish
5. a

Page 47
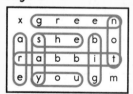

Page 48
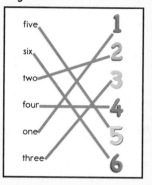

Page 49

Page 50
1. two   2. six
3. one   4. four
5. five   6. three

Page 51
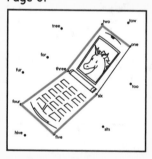

Page 52

Page 53

Page 54
1. doll   2. ball
3. girl   4. boy
5. toy

Page 55

Page 57
1. play   2. get
3. ride   4. go
5. work

Page 58
1. play   2. get
3. go   4. work
5. ride

Page 59
1. go   2. play
3. get   4. ride

Page 60
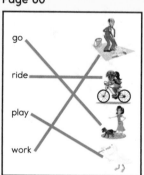

Answers

Page 61

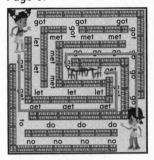

Page 62

4. Now we can play!
3. Get the brown rabbit.
1. Get the red toy.
2. Get the big ball.

Page 63

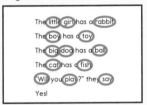

The little girl has a rabbit.
The boy has a toy.
The big dog has a ball.
The cat has a fish.
"Will you play?" they say.
Yes!

Page 64

two three doll
ball girl five

Page 65

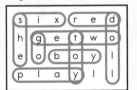

s i x r e d
h g e t w o
e o b o y l
p l a y l l

Page 67

1. make   2. give
3. look   4. like
5. want

Page 68

book   lick
make
give   look
want   like
want   live

Page 69

1. want   2. give
3. like   4. make
5. look

Page 70

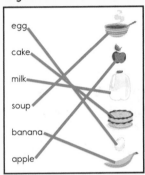

egg
cake
milk
soup
banana
apple

Page 71

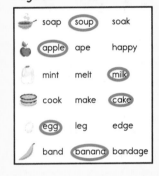

egg cake milk soup banana apple

Page 72

2. He put in milk.
4. Look! A cake!
1. I put in an egg.
3. She put in a banana.

Page 73

Have someone check
your answers.

Page 74

egg   cake   milk
soup   banana   apple

Page 75

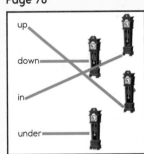

soap   (soup)   soak
(apple)   ape   happy
mint   melt   (milk)
cook   make   (cake)
(egg)   leg   edge
band   (banana)   bandage

Page 77

1. out   2. up
3. down   4. on
5. under

Page 78

up
down
in
under

Page 79

1. down   2. under
3. in   4. on
5. up

Page 80

Page 81

2. The turtle went in the water.
4. The turtle stuck out his head to
   say "Good-bye!"
3. The turtle went under the water.
1. The bird sat on the turtle.

Page 82

live   (give)   go
town   dawn   (down)
(look)   lock   book
(up)   pup   under
make   (cake)   cook

Page 85

1. make   2. look
3. under   4. like

Page 88

1. for   2. yes
3. but   4. no
5. and

Page 89

and   so
but
for   sand
no
cut   yes
      do

Page 91

1. do   2. have
3. has   4. my
5. be

Answers

Page 92

I have four legs.

She has a doll.

I do not have fur.

Yes, my bird is green.

Page 93
1. do
2. my
3. be
4. was

Page 94

Page 95

Page 96

feet   leg   eyes

hand   head

Page 97

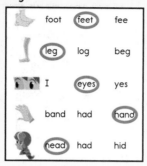

foot   (feet)   fee

(leg)   log   beg

I   (eyes)   yes

band   had   (hand)

(head)   had   hid

Page 98
4. But only one hand!
1. I see a head.
3. I see lots of feet.
2. I see eyes.

Page 99
1. eyes
2. head
3. leg
4. feet
5. hand

Page 100

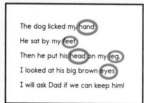

The dog licked my (hand)
He sat by my (feet)
Then he put his (head) on my (leg)
I looked at his big brown (eyes)
I will ask Dad if we can keep him!

Page 101

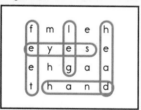

f	m	l	e	h
e	y	e	s	e
e	h	g	a	a
t	h	a	n	d

Page 102

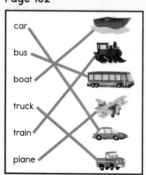

car
bus
boat
truck
train
plane

Page 103
Have someone check
your answers.

Page 104

cat   (car)   can

(bus)   but   was

coat   bit   (boat)

trick   tuck   (truck)

rain   (train)   tan

(plane)   plan   plate

Page 105
2. The truck went on the train.
4. But I went on the plane!
1. The car went on the truck.
3. The train went on the boat.

Page 106

car   bus   boat

truck   train   plane

Page 107

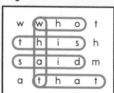

I put my (train) in a box.
I put in my (plane) too.
Then I put in a (car) and a (bus)
Mom put the box on the (truck)
"Wait!" I said.
I ran back into the house.
I almost forgot my (boat)

Page 110
1. what
2. that
3. saw
4. said
5. who

Page 111

w	(w	h	o)	t
(t	h	i	s)	h
(s	a	i	d)	m
a	(t	h	a	t)

Page 112
1. who
2. this
3. saw
4. said
5. what

Page 113

Page 114

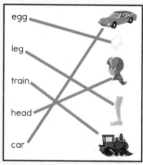

egg
leg
train
head
car

Page 115
1. head
2. who
3. that
4. boat

Page 116